# DIRECTOR'S CHOICE
# CHURCHES OF THE CHURCH OF ENGLAND

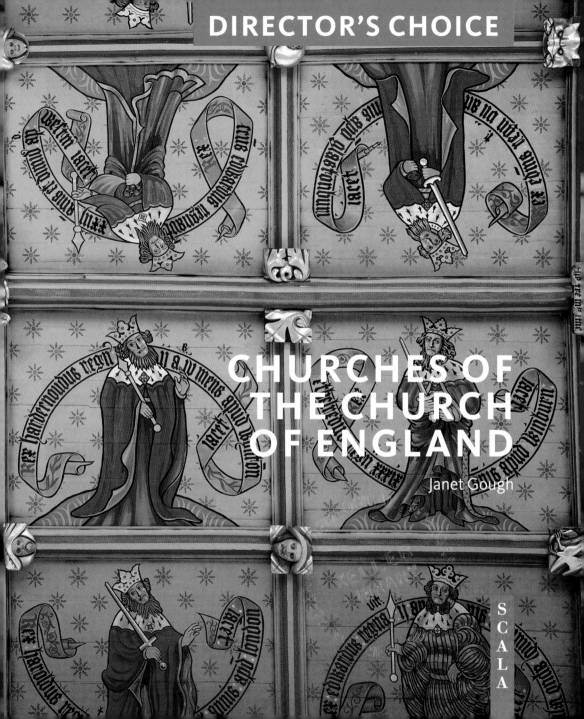

# CHURCHES OF THE CHURCH OF ENGLAND

Janet Gough

SCALA

# Foreword

ENGLAND'S PARISH CHURCHES are an integral and hugely significant part of its history and landscape. There are thousands of them – the Church of England alone is responsible for around 16,000. They are of immense architectural importance: some 78 per cent of the above 16,000 are listed and 45 per cent of Grade I listed buildings are churches. They are unique guardians of art and culture whilst at the same time, being repositories of the stories of the communities in which they stand, the vast majority remain active centres of service to those communities. They represent, in short, a priceless treasure of immeasurable worth to our nation.

Some of the churches in this delightful little book – like St Mary Redcliffe in Bristol – are well known. Most others, though they deserve to be, are not and Janet Gough has done a wonderful job in drawing attention to them here. I hope that these pages will whet the appetite of all who read them to explore further since, for every gem to which attention is drawn here, there are myriad other wonders waiting to be discovered and enjoyed.

I hope, too, that this book will help this precious part of our national heritage to be as highly valued as it ought: there is a pressing need for more help for the often small number of worshippers who care for them on everyone's behalf to be forthcoming. I hope, finally, that these pages might encourage their readers not only to relish the glorious architecture and history of our churches, but speak to them of the Living God revealed in Jesus Christ, to whose glory they were built.

THE RT REVD DR JOHN INGE
Bishop of Worcester
The Church of England's lead bishop for cathedrals
and church buildings

# THE CHURCH OF ENGLAND'S CHURCHES

CHRISTIANITY ARRIVED on these shores in the minds and hearts of individual Romans during the first and second centuries AD. It took only tenuous hold alongside other cults and the Romans left no complete Christian buildings behind them. Our earliest surviving churches date from the mid-seventh century and were built to support the work of missionaries, spreading Christianity from Ireland via the North-East and from Rome after 597, when St Augustine arrived in Canterbury.

At the Synod of Whitby in 664, England adopted the international Roman system of dioceses, initially roughly coterminous with Saxon kingdoms. The dioceses were headed by bishops, each with a mother church or cathedral (see the companion book in this series, *Cathedrals of the Church of England*). The Romans also gave us a basic model for church buildings, using the basilica form with a rounded end or apse to accommodate the altar, sometimes also with transepts.

Christianity flourished in Anglo-Saxon times, usually under royal patronage, notably that of Alfred the Great, but faced challenges, including the Viking raids. William the Conqueror and the Norman invasion finally established Christianity as the national religion in England and the Normans undertook extensive church building. In addition to the huge cathedrals in the new Romanesque or Norman style, William's feudal lords were encouraged to establish local parish churches. The pattern of the local lord of the manor commissioning and supporting the parish church continued well into the twentieth century (for example, the Smith banking dynasty built Waterford Church, p. 76, in 1872). It also explains

ABOVE: Choir at St Paul's, Birmingham (p. 62).

PREVIOUS PAGES: Medieval painted Kings' Ceiling at Beverley St Mary (p. 30).

why some aristocratic owners felt they could move the parish church (including St Lawrence, Mereworth, p. 54, and St Peter, Edensor, on the Chatsworth estate, p. 70).

Church buildings also changed radically with the introduction of the new pointed-arch or Gothic style from 1200 onwards. This was an engineering as well as a style issue, as Gothic buildings relied less on solid walls and more on principles of pressure and counter pressure, which in turn freed up walls for wonderful window schemes such as at Fairford (p. 42).

The Norman Conquest speeded up the establishment of great European-style monastic foundations, initially by the Benedictines (Beverley Minster, p. 30, and Wymondham Abbey, p. 22) and later the Augustinians (St Germans, p. 14) and other orders. Relations were not always perfect between monastic communities and local townsfolk; witness the feuding at Wymondham where two towers were built, one by the monks and the other by the town.

ABOVE: Oil on panel retable, St Mary's Church, Thornham Parva: the most significant extant fourteenth-century English oil painting. Recently conserved by the Hamilton Kerr Institute, Cambridge University, it is now securely presented daily at no charge in a tiny church in Suffolk.

OPPOSITE:
Music in St Germans, Cornwall (p. 14), in front of the east window containing stained glass made by William Morris's Merton Abbey studio, London, to Sir Edward Burne-Jones's design, 1895.

Henry VIII's dissolution of the monasteries and the subsequent break with Rome and the Reformation from the 1530s on saw several of these monastic foundations transformed into new cathedrals; many more, or parts of many, became parish churches.

Almost all churches were affected by over a hundred years of systematic iconoclasm or image-breaking brought about by extremist reformers, under Henry VIII's son, Edward VI, and later under Oliver Cromwell, the regicide ruler of the Commonwealth. Remarkable Pre-Reformation survivals include the Beauchamp Chapel in Warwick parish church (p. 39), with its painted stone-carved figures around the window jambs, and the magnificent stained glass of King's College Cambridge (p. 44), which was saved from Cromwell's iconoclasts apparently only by the intervention of John Milton, who was a fellow of King's.

Renaissance ideas and classicism had an impact on church building from the late sixteenth century onwards, though less than in other countries, perhaps because classicism was associated with Catholicism, and during the century of religious uncertainty from the mid-sixteenth to mid-seventeenth centuries few new churches were built. Nonetheless, this book includes wonderful examples of experimentation with new styles inspired by the Grand Tour (Mereworth, p. 54), Strawberry Hill Gothick (Shobdon, p. 58), the Arts and Crafts Movement (St Andrew, Roker, p. 82) and, in our own century, the prizewinning Ripon College Chapel at Cuddesdon, completed in 2013 (p. 92).

The Reformed Church's emphasis on the Word and preaching brought pulpits to the fore (see the triple-decker pulpits at Orton, p. 60, and Shobdon, p. 58). The nineteenth century return to a pre-Reformation emphasis on Incarnation and the celebration of Communion led to a glorious period of chancel building and decoration, as in nineteenth-century architect Henry Woodyer's two churches at Hascombe (p. 69) and Waterford (p. 76).

England's church legacy of art and artefacts created for the glory of God, divine service and commemoration is unique. The Thornham Parva retable is the tip of the iceberg; look in this book and beyond for countless stunning examples of world-class vernacular art, from medieval brasses and wall paintings (Trotton, p. 27) to John Rysbrack's monuments in Great Witley (p. 57) and St Germans (p. 15). These treasures also tell many stories. ChurchCare's '100 Church Treasures' campaign aims to conserve some of England's most significant church treasures.

ABOVE AND OPPOSITE: Washburn Heritage Centre, Fewston, North Yorkshire.

Week in, week out fine music is produced in church buildings, alluded to in the several exceptional organs in churches in this book, the carved musician capitals at Beverley St Mary (p. 30) and the painted gallery for the church band at Mereworth (p. 55).

Financial support from the government for churches is not a new idea. The building of new churches was encouraged by government-funded initiatives in the eighteenth century (see St Alfege in Greenwich, p. 53) and in the nineteenth century to address the shortage of church buildings, particularly in newly industrial areas. St George, Chorley, in Lancashire (p. 64) is one such, and its architect, Thomas Rickman the antiquarian, also devised our system of Gothic architectural classification.

Today church buildings are homes for worshipping congregations, bases for missional activity and often provide much-

needed support to the surrounding community. To do this better, many church communities seek to introduce WCs, kitchens and improved, more environmentally sound energy and heat (see www.shrinkingthefootprint.org). ChurchCare, the Church of England's national resource supporting church buildings and those caring for them, works hard with dioceses to ensure that adaptations are of the highest quality. A modest stone porch might be used to house a WC, for example, and there may be the opportunity for bold and beautiful statements about the vital part that the church can play in the community, or to give a new lease of life to a church, often thanks to funding made by The Heritage Lottery Fund.

St James, West Hampstead, in London, houses a café, post office and children's play area in a skilful adaptation that sits comfortably alongside an east end dedicated to regular worship. The organic form of the Washburn Heritage Centre connects Fewston Church to its hillside site: the Centre is run by volunteers to celebrate the heritage of the Washburn Valley (for information on visiting churches see www.churchdays.co.uk). All these developments are encouraged as part of ChurchCare's Open and Sustainable campaign so that a new generation can enjoy our magnificent heritage of church buildings.

*St Cedd's remote Celtic mission church*

# Chapel of St Peter-on-the-Wall or ad Vincula, Bradwell-on-Sea (Diocese of Chelmsford)

650s: one of the earliest surviving church buildings in England

Open daily; see website for details

www.bradwellchapel.org

Postcode: CM0 7PY

St Peter's chapel is an isolated single-cell building, with few windows and a backdrop of the flat Essex coast.

King Sigbert of the East Saxons asked the Irish-trained monks of Lindisfarne to send a Christian mission to Essex. So in 653 Cedd, later to become bishop of the East Saxons, sailed from Northumbria and landed on the peninsula at Bradwell, where he set up a monastic community in the ruins of the Roman fort. His stone church used materials from the fort: inside the chapel the Roman tiles that originally formed the chancel arch are still visible. Cedd's church was modelled with a round-ended or apsidal east end still marked in the ground.

Bede tells us that Cedd went out from Bradwell to establish other Christian centres at Mersea, Tilbury and Upminster. Later Cedd became interpreter at the Synod of Whitby (664), where the decision was taken to follow the Roman and not the Celtic tradition of Christianity in England, so this church is a rare survival of the Celtic Christian Church in England.

William the Conqueror's Domesday survey recorded a settled community around the chapel, but during the Middle Ages this moved inland, leaving the chapel isolated. For three hundred years it was used as a barn. In 1920 the chapel was restored as a Christian place of worship and taken under the care of Chelmsford Cathedral: today a chaplain conducts Eucharist services, special Sunday evening services in the summer and there are many informal events. Always open and much visited by walkers, St Peter's is a Christian place of sending out 'formed in order to be sent', just as in St Cedd's time.

ABOVE: St Peter's was one of the first churches to complete its roof repairs with funding from the Government's Listed Places of Worship Roof Repair Fund, with beautiful specially commissioned tiles.

RIGHT: It is a gentle half-mile walk to the church.

*Saintly foundation in an evocative coastal setting*

# St Aidan, Bamburgh (Diocese of Newcastle)

On the site of a wooden church, founded in 635 by St Aidan,
rebuilt and extended in the medieval period

Open daily 8.30am to dusk
www.staidan-bamburgh.co.uk
Postcode (vicarage): NE69 7DB

NORTHUMBRIA IS STEEPED in the history of British Christianity:
once traversed by our early saints, a sense of ancient spirituality
still survives along the wild coast. Lindisfarne, or Holy Island, is
famous for its Celtic priory; Jarrow Priory was the home of the
Venerable Bede.

Perhaps less familiar is Bamburgh. It was here that St Aidan,
founder of Lindisfarne, died in 651. The church lies on the long-
distance St Oswald's Way and its door is open every day to
pilgrims and to tourists visiting the picturesque village, once
seat of the Kings of Northumbria.

Today's church is not the one that St Aidan knew,
although a forked roof beam in the baptistery at the west end
is said to be an ancient remnant of his church. Otherwise it
was rebuilt and altered throughout the medieval period.

The nave with its pointed arcade is spacious and elegant;
just one of the capitals carries a stylised floral carving.
The late thirteenth-century chancel is surprisingly large,
contributing to the sprawling impression of the church
from outside. An impressive Victorian stone reredos by
local church architect W.S. Hicks provides a roll-call of
Northumberland saints, while a modern shrine surmounted
by gilded angels commemorates St Aidan.

A later association is with Grace Darling, the daughter
of a local lighthouse keeper, who helped rescue passengers
from a shipwrecked paddle steamer in 1838. A sign by her tomb
effigy in the north aisle requests 'Before you go, remember to say
a prayer for all sailors and those in danger on the sea' – a poignant
reminder of the difficulties faced by the seafarers who have long
worshipped in this isolated coastal church.

ABOVE: The memorial
to Grace Darling in the
north aisle. She is also
commemorated in a
stained-glass window
and a memorial in
the churchyard.

*Twelfth-century priory church on the site of the first Saxon cathedral of Cornwall*

# Priory Church of St Germanus, St Germans (Diocese of Truro)

Pre-Conquest foundation, twelfth century with eighteenth-century monuments

Open daily 10am to 4pm
www.stgermansparishes.com
Postcode: PL12 5LY

ONE OF THE OLDEST and finest historic churches of Cornwall, the church of St Germanus is on the site of the county's first cathedral. According to a twelfth-century chronicle, the Saxon king Athelstan personally appointed Bishop Conan here in 926 as part of his efforts to create a single kingdom of England. The church was rebuilt by the Normans as an Augustinian Priory in the early 1100s, after the bishop's seat was moved to Exeter.

The present church building preserves more original Norman masonry in its powerful and iconic west front, with its commanding twin towers, than any other Cornish church, and it is one of the best-preserved examples of its type anywhere. Today it is the honorary seat of the Bishop of St Germans and is also the local parish church. The building is looked after by the St Germans Priory Trust, which is working to improve the visitor welcome and provide more information about this fascinating place.

The church stands directly adjacent to Port Eliot, a fine eighteenth-century stately home designed by Sir John Soane, which was developed out of the priory buildings after the Reformation. The church contains a memorial plaque to Sir John Eliot, local MP and a major figure in the development of parliamentary democracy, who was imprisoned for his defiance by Charles I in the Tower of London; he died there in 1632. There is also a superb monument to his son, Edward Eliot MP, by John Rysbrack.

RIGHT: One of Flemish sculptor John Rysbrack's (1694–1770) earliest commissions after his arrival in England in 1720, showing Edward Eliot MP on a sarcophagus with a mourner, perhaps his wife.

This exceptional ensemble of buildings is set within a glorious park designed by Humphry Repton on the Tamar Estuary, part of the Lower Tamar Area of Outstanding Natural Beauty. The church therefore provides the focus for a rewarding visit.

*Remote island church on the bank of the River Swale*

## St Thomas the Apostle, Isle of Harty, Sheppey (Diocese of Canterbury)

Late eleventh-century origin, restored in 1878–80 by Joseph Clark

Open daily

www.achurchnearyou.com/harty-st-thomas-the-apostle

Postcode: ME12 4BQ

THE OPEN DOOR at Harty, combined with the sense of discovery at finding a church 3 miles off the main road, contributes to this church's charm. Set in a peaceful remote position in the south-eastern corner of the Isle of Sheppey, overlooking the River Swale and surrounded by mudflats and waterways, this is a haven for birdwatchers and for visitors seeking peace and sanctuary.

The church leaflet quotes a letter from Sir John Betjeman apologising for his absence: 'I shall have to console myself with memories of the church in its splendid isolation, with sea birds wheeling by and the Thames so wide as to be open sea, and air so fresh as to be healthier than yoghurt.'

On approach this little building, with low-tiled eaves and stumpy shingled fifteenth-century west tower (supported internally by a wooden frame), is backlit by a shimmering expanse of water. St Thomas's doesn't boast the architectural grandeur of the island's other churches, yet a round-headed north window and a south door, both now blocked, attest to its eleventh-century foundation.

Although the church is much restored, the atmosphere inside is enhanced by oil lamps: there is no electricity. A mid-fourteenth-century wooden rood screen separates the chancel, where, set in the east wall, is a late fourteenth-century gabled and pinnacled niche. Contents include a Flemish wood chest, stolen and returned in the 1980s, carved with figures of jousting knights, and two hidden brasses.

ABOVE: Fourteenth-century chancel screen in the nave. Evidence of volcanic tufa stone, rarely used after the early Norman period, demonstrates the Norman and possibly earlier origins of this and many other churches.

Historically the priest was rowed by ferry to this secluded spot from the mainland. This is a rural church with challenges, like many others, yet it is valued by its island community, many of whom choose to marry here. A service is held each month and the church is opened daily by its few neighbours.

*One of only four surviving round churches built by Crusaders*

# Church of the Holy Sepulchre, Northampton (Diocese of Peterborough)

From 1100

Additional opening hours Wednesday and Saturday 2pm to 4pm (May to September)

www.stseps.org

Postcode: NN1 3NL 🐦 @Seps1

SIMON DE SENLIS, Earl of Northampton, returned from the first Crusade in 1099 and built his round church, inspired by the Emperor Constantine's Church of the Holy Sepulchre in Jerusalem, which marks the spot of Christ's crucifixion. Round churches, such as the Temple Church in London, are more often associated with the Knights Hospitaller or Templar who guarded the Holy Sepulchre in Jerusalem; but St Sep's, as it is known locally, has always been a parish church.

Originally the nave consisted of the circular 'crusader round' with eight massive Norman columns and a small projecting chancel to the east. No doubt because of structural problems, it was significantly altered in the thirteenth and fourteenth centuries, giving the circular arcade its pointed arches, raising the roof and creating a much longer projecting nave and chancel, eventually with aisles to the east. Around 1400 the west end tower was built.

In the nineteenth century Sir George Gilbert Scott restored the church, adding the apsidal east end. At that time several stained-glass windows were introduced, including work by Morris & Co., Kempe, and the Jaffa window commemorating Richard I in 1192 and the Northamptonshire regiment.

St Sep's has a strong tradition as a military church. The beautiful south-east regimental chapel, 'the Warriors' Chapel', was dedicated in 1921. Following conservation of the Victorian paintings, new lighting and chairs, it was rededicated 'the Soldiers' Chapel' and is covered in brass plaques to remind us of those who have made the final sacrifice.

ABOVE: Exterior view of the circular nave, dating from 1100, and west end tower of *c*.1400.

OPPOSITE: Crusader round nave with its massive cylindrical Norman piers and later pointed arches.

Over the past 25 years the small congregation has done a remarkable job raising over £1.2 million to conserve the building. The church hosts concerts and plays and pre-arranged tours, and is open on two afternoons a week in the summer but is planning to open more. It deserves to be better known.

*Church of former Norman priory with superb carved west doorway*

# St Bees, Priory Church of St Mary and St Bega (Diocese of Carlisle)

Norman origin, restored in the seventeenth and nineteenth centuries

Open 8.30am to 7.30pm

www.stbeespriory.org.uk

Postcode: CA27 0DR

THE PRIORY CHURCH of St Bees is one of the finest Grade I medieval buildings in the north-west of England. Originally a Benedictine priory (1120), little remains of the old priory buildings but much of the church itself, such as the pillars and north transept, is original and in regular use today. The splendid Norman west doorway is an exceptional survival.

According to legend, the priory was established by a Christian Irish princess fleeing an enforced marriage to a Viking. Following the Dissolution in 1539, the church continued to be used by the parish. Restoration took place in 1622, and again in 1816 with the founding of a theological college, the first outside Oxford and Cambridge, at which time the roofless original chancel area was restored. William Butterfield carried out further restoration between 1870 and 1899. As part of this, stained glass by William Wailes was added showing Old and New Testament stories. An ornamental iron screen was also installed. In 2012 the original chancel and later theological college classroom was fully restored.

The south transept houses an organ of cathedral proportions and exceptional quality. It is one of the last to be built (1899) under the personal supervision of the famous 'Father' Henry Willis.

OPPOSITE: Fine Norman west doorway, 1150–60, with round arches on pillars in the thickness of the wall, the arches carved with beakheads and chevrons.

The discovery in 1981 of the almost perfectly preserved body of a medieval knight, now known as 'St Bees Man', was one of the most extraordinary archaeological burial finds in Britain in the late twentieth century. The story of this find and of much of the history of the church, St Bees School and the village is told in its heritage exhibitions in the aisles.

The church is preparing for its 900th anniversary with a 'Vision 2020' plan. The vision is to build mission in the community and broaden the church's styles of worship.

*Substantial medieval church unharmoniously shared by town and monks*

# Wymondham Abbey (Diocese of Norwich)

Dating from early twelfth century with fifteenth-century towers
and new interpretation centre

Additional opening hours Monday to Saturday 10am to 5pm, Sunday 12 noon to 5pm
www.wymondhamabbey.org.uk
Postcode: NR18 0PH

RECORDED IN THE Domesday Book, Wymondham (pronounced
Wyndham) town and church have existed since at least Saxon times.
A Benedictine daughter of one of England's earliest abbeys, St Albans,
Wymondham Abbey was founded in 1107.

The church has a fine Norman nave topped by a hammerbeam roof
with angels and star-shaped bosses. A gilded reredos, of Christ in glory
surrounded by three tiers of biblical characters and saints in intricate
niches, with a projecting tester, was designed by Sir Ninian Comper in
1912 and gives the long nave light and brightness.

Throughout the Middle Ages the monks and townspeople
fought over ownership and use of the church; in 1249 Pope
Innocent determined a settlement whereby the town took
responsibility for the nave and north aisle. As at Ely Cathedral,
the monks replaced their crossing tower in the late thirteenth
century with a new octagonal tower straying a couple of bays
into the nave; this antagonised the townsfolk, who some forty
years later responded by building an even taller tower at the
West End.

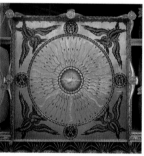

Opened in November 2015, a major scheme, part-funded by
the Heritage Lottery Fund, has added two new extensions on
the east end in the footprint of former monastic buildings. The medieval
fabric is attractively complemented by oak, lead and glass to create new
facilities, including meeting rooms, WCs and an education space.

ABOVE: Tester to Sir
Ninian Comper's nave
reredos.

OPPOSITE: Wymondham
Abbey Church sits
in an oasis of green,
dominated by two late
medieval towers, with
monastic ruins and an
east end extension.

Most exciting was the discovery in a window arch, revealed for
the first time since the Dissolution of the Monasteries, of a medieval
bar tracery design incised in the stonework. This drawing of a Gothic
window with a central rose over a pair of two light windows was found
over a large double circle and numerous graffiti, including daisywheel
designs, a ship and a grotesque head.

*A Norman soldier bishop's church for the oldest charitable institution in England*

# St Cross Church, The Hospital of the Holy Cross and Almshouse of Noble Poverty (Diocese of Winchester)

Main church building late Norman/Transitional, 1158–1250

Open daily in summer, closed on Sundays in winter except for church services (see website for opening times)
www.hospitalofstcross.co.uk/the-church  🐦@hospitalofstx
Postcode: SO23 9SD

A VIEW ACROSS the water meadows of the massive Norman cruciform church of St Cross takes you back to the early Middle Ages and the terrible civil war between Matilda (daughter of Henry I and mother of the future Henry II) and King Stephen, brother of Henry of Blois, who founded St Cross in the 1130s, and into the reign of Henry II.

Henry, Bishop of Winchester and grandson of William the Conqueror, founded the hospital of the Holy Cross for 13 poor men (the 'Black Brothers' who wear a distinctive Jerusalem cross). In the fifteenth century Cardinal Beaufort, son of the powerful John of Gaunt, Duke of Lancaster, and his mistress Katherine Swinford, added the Almshouse of Noble Poverty (for 35 'Red Brothers'), and from 1509 the church has also been a parish church. As a lay foundation, St Cross never suffered Reformation plundering by Henry VIII and in spite of ups and downs, some fictionally chronicled by Anthony Trollope in the nineteenth century, the foundation continues to thrive today.

ABOVE: View towards the east end showing beautiful Transitional elements of pointed clerestory arches and rib vaulting above round arches and slim attached piers decorating great Norman pillars.

Inside the surprisingly lofty church the massive Norman pillars, round arches and ubiquitous chevron decoration give way gradually to a more Transitional style using pointed arches. There are many hints of medieval wall painting, from masonry patterns to fragments of a narrative scene using expensive malachite and lapis lazuli. Recently the fine Renaissance choir stalls, with fretwork, roundels and animated figures, have been conserved and reassembled.

Today Beaufort's fifteenth-century range remains inhabited by 25 lay brothers. The medieval tradition of hospitality continues at the Porter's Lodge, where any visitor can request Wayfarer's Dole (these days a small helping of beer and bread) free of charge; the excellent café in the Hundred Men's Hall serves coffee and cake. There is a small charge for admission.

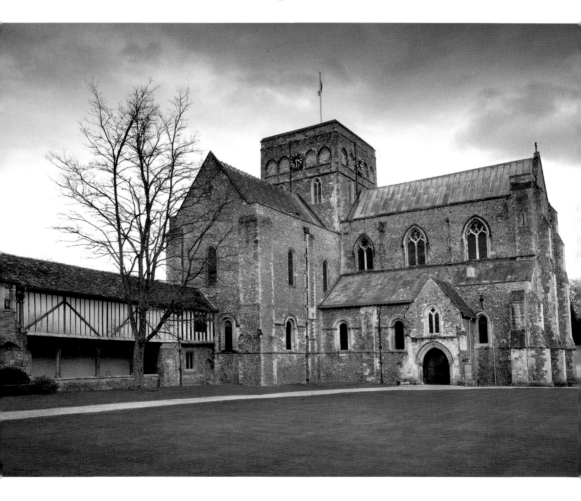

*Unassuming parish church with significant brasses and wall paintings*

# St George, Trotton (Diocese of Chichester)

Constructed around 1300 in the Early English style

Open daily
www.achurchnearyou.com/trotton-st-george
Postcode: GU31 5EN

TROTTON PARISH CHURCH, beside the river Rother, is virtually unaltered since its construction. The Early English tower has thin lancet windows topped by a low, shingled splayed-foot spire. The church is a single oblong space with no aisles, clerestory or chancel divider (stone corbels suggest an earlier rood screen), and four bays with geometric tracery windows: a quatrefoil above two trefoiled lancets. The wooden roof survives with tie-beams, arch braces and collars.

The simplicity of the church is offset by fourteenth-century wall paintings, first rediscovered and revealed in 1904, covering the west end and parts of the north and south walls. The west wall (opposite) is a red monochrome Judgement Scene dominated by Christ sitting on a rainbow, above Moses with the Tablets of the Law. Underneath is Evil Man surrounded by the Seven Deadly Sins issuing from the jaws of dragons, and Good Man, in fourteenth-century dress, surrounded by roundels of the Seven Acts of Mercy, with a circular consecration cross at his right foot.

Set in the nave floor is England's earliest surviving full-size female brass, of Lady Margaret Camoys (died 1310). A little hair escapes the tight triangle of her wimple and the naturalism of late Early English art is evident in the fall of her robes over her swaying right leg.

Grander and more stylised is the double brass of Thomas Lord Camoys and his wife. Set under a beautiful double ogee-shaped cusped canopy, this is one of the largest and best-preserved brass monuments in the country. Thomas Camoys commanded Henry V's left flank at the Battle of Agincourt in 1415. The church celebrated this anniversary with the current Lord Camoys in 2015.

ABOVE: Brass of Thomas Lord Camoys (died 1419) and his wife on top of a stone tomb chest, decorated with shields and quatrefoils, directly in front of the altar.

# Collegiate Church of St Mary, Ottery St Mary (Diocese of Exeter)

Collegiate foundation of the fourteenth century
Open daily
www.otterystmary.org.uk
Postcode: EX11 1DU

ALTHOUGH OTTERY ST MARY is now a parish church serving its eponymous delightful rural town, the building was originally envisioned by Bishop John Grandisson (Bishop of Exeter 1327–69) on the scale of a small cathedral to house a college of secular priests. The fine ensemble of buildings around the church, including a house that was the birthplace of Samuel Taylor Coleridge, still gives the impression of a cathedral close.

The scale and quality of the church will surprise the casual visitor and confuse those with a knowledge of architectural history. Despite being completely built in the mid-fourteenth century, stylistically it appears wholly a century earlier, in the Early English style. This conundrum has exercised scholars for generations: many thought Grandisson must have adapted an earlier building. According to recent research, the main reason for this appears to be that the masons had previously worked on Wells Cathedral, which has clear similarities, and were also working within the local Devon style, which remained simple throughout the fourteenth century. The church has little stylistically in common with the cathedral at Exeter, which Grandisson was also developing; however, some plan features are copied, such as the transept towers. It is as if Grandisson wanted his big collegiate church to look rustic in comparison with his grand metropolitan cathedral.

OPPOSITE: North aisle fan vaulting, 1520, with five pendant bosses on stems, one twisted, showing a flower opening up.

The interior, however, is very ornate, with original misericords, screens and vaulting, and later fan-vaulting in the sixteenth-century north aisle. The south transept houses an extraordinary astronomical clock, a gift of Bishop Grandisson, several of whose relatives are commemorated in the church with elaborate monuments.

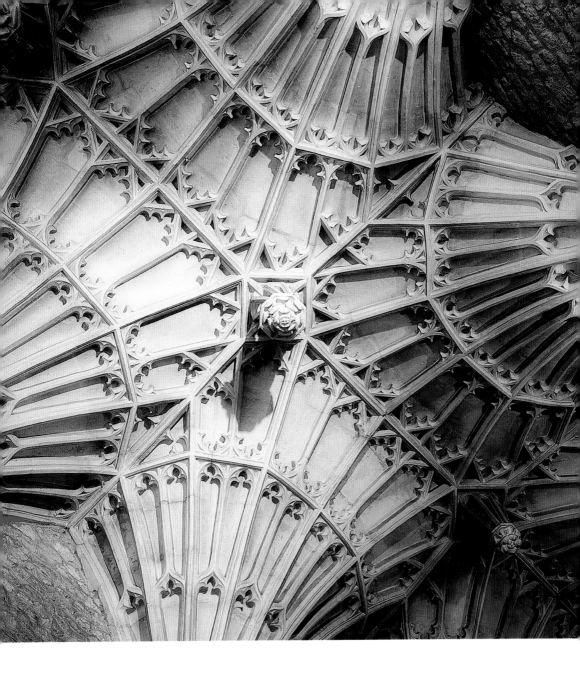

*Two vast medieval churches within one small market town*

## Beverley Minster, the Parish Church of St John and St Martin (Diocese of York)

Eighth-century foundation; mainly thirteenth and fifteenth centuries

Open daily 9am to 5.30pm in summer, 9am to 4pm in winter
www.beverleyminster.org.uk  🐦@Bev_Minster
Postcode: HU17 ODP

## St Mary, Beverley (Diocese of York)

Twelfth, fourteenth and fifteenth centuries

Open Monday to Saturday 11am to 3pm
www.stmarysbeverley.org  🐦@StMarysBeverley
Postcode: HU17 8DL

BEVERLEY IS A medieval market town blessed with two historic parish churches of remarkable size, beauty and significance. Traditionally they have fulfilled different roles, the Minster of St John providing civic services and a ministry to the wider region, St Mary's catering for the local community. Now the two churches are working together more closely than ever before to realise the potential of these extraordinary buildings.

Standing at the southern edge of the historic town, the Minster Church of St John, although now a parish church, retains much of the prestige of its former status as a place of pilgrimage. The church is cruciform, with large transepts and twin towers that can be seen for miles around. Mostly thirteenth century but including the fifteenth-century Percy Chapel, it is

OPPOSITE: Beverley Minster, nave.

BELOW: Beverley Minster and St Mary's church seen from the racecourse to the south of the town.

considered one of the finest examples of medieval church architecture in the country. Treasures include the Frith Stool, associated with St John of Beverley himself, who founded the original monastery here in the eighth century, as well as carvings of medieval musicians, misericords, stained glass and a huge treadmill crane.

St Mary's is located just within the medieval north gate in the Georgian Quarter of the town. This church was founded in the twelfth century and richly endowed by the citizens and town guilds. It was enlarged in the fourteenth and fifteenth centuries and the tower was rebuilt in the early sixteenth century following its collapse. Highlights include the medieval painted Kings' Ceiling (illustrated on pp. 2–3), misericords, the splendidly vaulted St Michael's Chapel, a rabbit carving said to have inspired Lewis Carroll's White Rabbit, and the Priest's Room, which contains a small but fascinating museum that has been described as a 'cabinet of curiosities'. Access to the museum needs to be arranged beforehand.

*Parish church on a monumental scale with spectacular tower visible for miles*

## St Botolph, Boston (Diocese of Lincoln)

Fourteenth-century Perpendicular church with nineteenth-century furnishings

Open Monday to Saturday 8.30am to 4pm, Sunday 7.30am to 4pm

www.parish-of-boston.org.uk/church/st-botolphs

Postcode: PE21 6NW

AT THE END of the thirteenth century the wealth of Boston's merchants was almost as great as that of London's, thanks to a flourishing sea trade. A parish church on an exceptional scale was clearly required and St Botolph's remains to this day one of the largest and tallest in England.

Building started at the beginning of the fourteenth century and, despite its size, all but the tower was finished by the end of the century. The result is a uniformity of style within, which adds to the sense of space: and at 20,000 square feet, this is a very large space indeed.

The interior owes much to the Victorians, with its massed ranks of pews, tower vault, Gothic Revival east window and choir stall canopies. There is also much good stained glass by the renowned firms of Kempe Studios, Hardman & Co. and Burlison & Grylls. Sir Charles Nicholson added the painted timber nave ceiling in the early part of the twentieth century. Don't miss the remarkable late fourteenth-century misericords: the 62 misericords include a couple in their kitchen, a woman chasing a fox and a wolf preaching to hens.

The tower was added to in stages, although it seems that some may have had ambitions to build even higher: legend has it that the nickname 'The Stump' originates from the fact that a planned steeple was never built.

The church is playing a leading role in the regeneration of the town. Notices on the church website are in six languages, and a new shop and café welcome visitors.

ABOVE: St Botolph's fourteenth-century tower stands 272 feet (80 metres) high and its distinctive octagonal lantern is visible for miles, as it would have been to medieval seafarers.

OPPOSITE: The east window with Decorated tracery.

*'The fairest, goodliest and most famous parish church in England' – Queen Elizabeth I*

# St Mary, Redcliffe (Diocese of Bristol)

Wealthy merchants' parish church, substantially rebuilt
in the fourteenth and fifteenth centuries

Additional opening times Monday to Saturday 8.30am to 5pm
www.stmaryredcliffe.co.uk  ✔@StMaryRedcliffe
Postcode: BS1 6NL

DOMINATING THE River Avon in Bristol, from where merchant ships
set sail first to Europe and eventually to the New World, St Mary
Redcliffe displays both baroque Decorated inventiveness and
upward-soaring Perpendicular architecture.

Facing the river, the spectacular north porch is a hexagonal
construction of the 1320s by the so-called Bristol Master, the
unnamed designer who may also have been responsible for
the equally unusual east end of Bristol Cathedral. Three-
dimensional nodding ogee niches are set around a cusped,
oriental-feeling arch, with lively carved figures on the
plinths and hidden in the bulbous decorative foliage, all the
rage from 1300. No-one quite understands the layout inside
the porch with its three entrances, but it was probably a
shrine to Our Lady to which pilgrims came.

Inside, the cruciform church has aisles along its transepts
and nave, a projecting Lady Chapel and stone vaulting with
hundreds of bosses throughout. Massive clerestory or upper
windows circle the church, surmounted by blind tracery that
further emphasises the building's verticality.

Rich patron William Canynges, MP and Mayor of Bristol,
died in 1474 and has two effigies in the church: one a
conventional funerary monument with his wife, the second
an alabaster monument of him as a priest – he was ordained
after his wife's death.

The church has a café in the undercroft. Ambitious plans are
afoot to carry out a conservation programme and re-open the
church's view over the quayside, from which so many set sail,
and re-establish its links with Brunel's great nineteenth-century
railway station.

ABOVE: Painted wooden statue
of Queen Elizabeth I, who
much admired the church.

OPPOSITE: Decorated north
porch, 1320s, perhaps once
a pilgrim shrine.

*Medieval church with fine craftsmanship in stone and timber*

# St Mary, Nantwich (Diocese of Chester)

Built 1340s–1360s in Decorated style, with Perpendicular additions

Open Monday to Saturday 9am to 5pm in summer, 9am to 4pm in winter
www.stmarysnantwich.org.uk
Postcode: CW5 5RQ

ST MARY'S CHURCH is at the centre of town life. This striking and intricate medieval masterpiece rises up from the green square of the historic market town of Nantwich. The doors are open wide to visitors daily throughout the year, and the church lies on the Two Saints Way, a 92-mile pilgrimage path established in 2012 running between the cathedral cities of Chester and Lichfield.

Commanding outside and voluminous inside, St Mary's is on a grand scale. Comparisons can be made with many of our cathedrals and, indeed, it is believed that the masons who built it also worked at Chester Cathedral. Started in the 1340s, works were halted by the Black Death, but most of the building seen today was completed by the 1380s. As a result, the style is predominantly Decorated, though there are later Perpendicular additions, including the two-storey south porch.

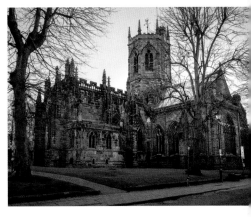

What catches the eye most from outside, even against all the flourishes and pinnacles, is the impressive octagonal crossing tower. The fourteenth-century choir stalls are a highlight of the interior: the carving of the triple-arched canopy is exquisite, whilst the characterful misericords offer considerable entertainment. One particular example shows why it was not a good idea to get on the wrong side of a medieval craftsman: the face that forms the rump of a carved dodo is reportedly the likeness of the vicar of the time.

OPPOSITE: Detail of the fourteenth-century choir stalls and canopies.

The parish here is exceptionally active, engaged in numerous community activities and dedicated to the care of its remarkable church. Conservation works have taken place in recent years and a sympathetic reordering was completed in 2016, introducing new facilities to support the continued mission of this fine church.

*Parish church with grand medieval chantry chapel*

## St Mary, Warwick (Diocese of Coventry)

Norman and late medieval, partly rebuilt after fire of 1694

Additional opening times Monday to Saturday 10am to 6pm, Sunday 12.30 to 4pm

www.stmaryswarwick.org.uk  🐦 @StMarysWarwick

Postcode: CV34 4RA

MAJESTICALLY POSITIONED at the highpoint of the pretty county town of Warwick, St Mary's Church is in two halves. The tall, spacious nave was rebuilt by contemporaries of Sir Christopher Wren after the town fire of 1694, and is finished off by a massive three-storey tower to the west of the nave.

The medieval church remains to the east of the nave. Above the Norman crypt is an integral fourteenth-century chapter house, unusual for a parish, albeit collegiate, church. The chancel, of the same era, was built by Thomas Beauchamp, who is buried with his wife under full-size alabaster effigies with alabaster weepers in contemporary costume around the chest. St Mary's other notable alabasters include a sixteenth-century tomb effigy of Ambrose, Earl of Warwick, laid out on his soldier's rush mat, and Robert Dudley, Earl of Leicester, favourite of Elizabeth I, buried alongside his third wife, Lettice, whose infant son is also buried in the Beauchamp Chapel.

The spectacular Beauchamp Chapel was built as a mausoleum to Richard Beauchamp, Earl of Warwick and friend of kings, to his detailed instructions. With the tomb chest at its centre, the chapel was designed as one piece and displays stained glass and carved and painted window tracery under lierne vaulting. Thankfully, the ensemble was little damaged by Reformation iconoclasts.

The tomb effigy of Richard Beauchamp is supported by gilt-bronze mourners set into his Purbeck marble tomb, including his son-in-law Richard Neville, Duke of Warwick, the infamous 'kingmaker'. Wealth and status are ephemeral: within ten years of Beauchamp's death his direct line was extinguished and the bloody Wars of the Roses were in full swing.

The church offers an excellent visitor welcome. When I visited, local primary school children were giving guided tours.

ABOVE: Tomb effigy of Richard Beauchamp (died 1439), looking up through open praying hands towards the ceiling boss of the Virgin Mary.

OPPOSITE: Glimpse into the Beauchamp Chapel. Note the fifteenth-century gilded and painted carved stone figures filling the window jambs.

*Church by ruins of a Benedictine Abbey, with fabulous seventeenth-century painted ceiling*

# St Peter and St Paul, Muchelney (Diocese of Bath and Wells)

Fifteenth-century Perpendicular

Open daily 10am to 6pm in summer, 10am to dusk in winter

www.achurchnearyou.com/muchelney

Postcode: TA10 0DQ

THE FORMER 'great island of Muchelney' came to national fame during flooding in 2014, when the village of Muchelney found itself surrounded by water once more and the church played a key part in the distribution of relief to the local community. Being at the highest point in the village, it was used to store and distribute food and newspapers, and acted as an emergency post office.

The church is substantially fifteenth-century, built of local Lias stone with Ham stone dressings. The fine three-stage tower is decorated with grotesques.

For many the chief glory of the church is the wooden-boarded wagon roof of the nave, decorated with early seventeenth-century paintings of angels, cherubs and clouds, with star panels at the east end with the sun in the centre.

One feature of the adjacent ruined abbey is now part of the church: thirteenth-century tiles with vivid patterned decoration are set into the sanctuary floor and near the fifteenth-century octagonal font. Although not unique, the barrel organ, dating from 1848, is rare. It was built in London by Gray & Davison. Such instruments replaced church bands of musicians in the nineteenth century.

Adjacent to the church, the sixteenth-century Abbot's Lodging and abbey ruins are now managed by English Heritage.

ABOVE: Vernacular seventeenth-century paintings of angels in the nave roof, some of them shockingly bare-breasted!

*Pure Perpendicular church with complete set of medieval glass*

# St Mary the Virgin, Fairford (Diocese of Gloucester)

'Wool church' of the 1490s

Open daily 10am to 5pm in summer, 10am to 4pm in winter

www.stmaryschurchfairford.org.uk

Postcode: GL7 4AF

THANKS TO THE great wealth generated by the Cotswolds wool industry, father and son wool merchants John and Edward Towe funded the complete rebuilding of St Mary the Virgin in the Perpendicular style, complete with a crossing tower guarded by dwarfs at its four corners and a cheeky late fifteenth-century youth climbing over the parapet.

The church is most celebrated for its complete scheme of stained-glass stories filling its 28 large Perpendicular windows.

Made between 1500 and 1515, the windows tell the story of St Mary the Virgin, of Christ and of the Church with a wonderful rogues' gallery of early sixteenth-century villains facing saints and martyrs in the clerestory. They are of remarkable quality, thought to be by a Flemish master working for the court, a notion reinforced by various references to characters in the courts of Henry VII and Henry VIII. Nobody knows how this glass survived the iconoclasts of the Reformation; it has recently benefited from an extensive restoration programme.

The excellent free audio guide very much enhances visitors' enjoyment and understanding of the windows, which give us an insight into the medieval religious mind. Window One uses typology, the prefiguration of New Testament events in the Old Testament (see also King's College Chapel overleaf). Eve is a reference to Mary, her purity prefigured in the story of Moses and the Burning Bush, when, despite the flames, the bush remained intact. The triumph of the scheme is the Last Judgement in the Great West Window.

OPPOSITE: Window one: the Fall, showing Eve disobeying God; Moses and the Burning Bush, symbolising Mary in her virginity; Gideon and the Fleece, foreshadowing the Incarnation of Christ; and the Presentation to King Solomon, thought to depict a Tudor royal princess.

## King's College Chapel, Cambridge (Diocese of Ely)

Fifteenth to early sixteenth century, late Perpendicular

Open most days (charge); see website for opening times
www.kings.cam.ac.uk/chapel  ✈@Kings_College
Postcode: CB2 1ST

CONCEIVED AND BEGUN by Henry VI in the 1440s as the chapel for the newest and largest college in Cambridge in the late Perpendicular Gothic style, King's College Chapel was completed 70 years later in the reign of King Henry VIII, who added the stained glass and carved oak screen and stalls in the Renaissance idiom.

Henry VI's Chapel, a tall, narrow, oblong building with no aisles, takes its inspiration from an earlier royal chapel, the now-demolished St Stephen's Chapel in Westminster. Master mason John Wastell, one of the great architects of the late English Perpendicular style, finished the chapel in 1515 and most famously designed the magnificent fan vaulting with its grounding four-centred transverse arches. Wastell's genius ensured the unity of the building, but Henry VIII's flamboyant dynastic decoration of roses, portcullises and heraldic beasts at the west end is a far cry from Henry VI's more restrained sculptural half-angels at the east end.

The great glass windows contain a sophisticated complete set of stained glass from the reign of Henry VIII. The iconography is typological, with each window depicting a scene from the New Testament (below) prefigured by scene in the Old Testament (above). The screen, commissioned when Anne Boleyn was queen, displays an exquisite flowering of the English Renaissance in its capitals, beasts and roundels. It was carved by French craftsmen in a northern mannerist style. The massive organ sitting above the screen dates from the 1630s.

Henry VI's original foundation included 16 choristers, and music has always been a significant part of chapel life. In 1918 King's held its first Festival of Nine Lessons and Carols, a service that has been broadcast every Christmas Eve bar one since 1928.

ABOVE: Half-angel with coat of arms of Henry VI.

OPPOSITE: Largest spanned fan vault above Flemish stained glass from the reign of Henry VIII.

*Rare new church for its era, with exceptional classically inspired furnishings*

# St Lawrence, Folke (Diocese of Salisbury)

Jacobean Gothic, 1628

Open at weekends; the noticeboard gives details of several key holders in the village.
www.threevalleysteam.org
Postcode: DT9 5HP

FOLKE CHURCH may well have sat at the centre of the village at one time, but now there is only a tiny hamlet nudging up against the churchyard to the north and the beautiful Dorset countryside stretching for miles around: the plague is thought to have been to blame.

Constructed on the site of an earlier chapel with Saxon origins, a little of which is visible in the tower, from afar it resembles any number of picturesque medieval parish churches, but come closer and the triplet square-headed windows hint at its real date. In fact St Lawrence is a rare example of Jacobean Gothic, built at a time when church building outside London had almost ceased following the upheaval of the Reformation.

Nowadays the exterior of the church looks more Gothic than was intended, thanks to the addition of battlements by the Victorians, but step inside and the influence of the classical shouts out from the extraordinary furnishings. Pew-ends sport scallops and reeded panels, the font cover has elaborate scrollwork and the pulpit a dentilled cornice. Most

ABOVE: Detail of strapwork scrolls on seventeenth-century timber chancel screen.

elaborate, and a feast for the eyes, are the timber screens. The Ionic pilasters of the chancel screen are crowned with strapwork scrolls and pinnacles; a smaller version in the north arcade once had a door that may have led to a family pew.

The church is full of interesting oddities. An ancient hourglass stand by the pulpit would once have ensured that sermons were not over-long, and the lectern is really a desk attached to the screen.

This tiny community is proud of its church and recently raised a considerable sum to re-roof it.

*Sir Christopher Wren's only rural church*

## St Mary the Virgin, Ingestre (Diocese of Lichfield)

Palladian Greek-design classical church, consecrated 1676

Open daily 10am to dusk
www.stmaryschurch-ingestre.co.uk
Postcode: ST18 0RF

THE PARISH CHURCH of St Mary was built by Walter Chetwynd, a member of the Royal Society. He was a friend of architect and Renaissance man Christopher Wren and the design of this classical church, a square beyond a square, with its balance of wood, plaster and natural light, reveals the hand of the master. Its distinctive pillars of four Doric columns topped by square springers are virtually identical to those in Wren's St Bride's Church, London. The barrel vault over the chancel and flat nave ceiling are superbly stuccoed in white plaster. Leafy swags and wreaths on the ceiling and screen celebrate the bounty of the countryside.

The church incorporates stained-glass roundels from the thirteenth-century church (a chapel of ease) that it replaced.

Visitors enter through a circular porch under a square bell tower into the square four-bayed arcaded nave. The eye is drawn to the square chancel, divided from the nave by a triple-arched wooden screen with fluted pilasters.

Great families living next door continued to support the church, leaving interesting monuments and stained glass, including a window by Burne-Jones. The church installed one of the first electric lighting schemes outside London and still uses the original Victorian wrought iron fittings.

Sadly, death-watch beetle closed the church for four years to 2004, but this was fixed with the help of a grant from the Heritage Lottery Fund, which also provided a further grant for the bells. Now the church is open daily to visitors and is in regular use for worship.

ABOVE: Magnificently carved royal coat of arms, perhaps by the Flemish master Grinling Gibbons, above the chancel screen. Replacing the rood, or Christ Crucified, of pre-Reformation churches, it acted as a powerful reminder that the Church of England was now Protestant, with the sovereign at its head.

*Waterfront church with organ once played by Handel*

# Holy Trinity, Gosport (Diocese of Portsmouth)

Late seventeenth century, with modifications in every subsequent century

Open most lunchtimes: see website for details

www.holytrinitygosport.co.uk

Postcode: PO12 1HL

STANDING ON THE waterfront at Gosport, Holy Trinity, with its fine campanile tower, watches over the entrance to Portsmouth Harbour.

First built in 1696 and enlarged in the eighteenth and nineteenth centuries, it was restored in 1887 by Sir Arthur Blomfield, who added the tower. The exterior looks like an Italianate red brick basilica. Inside, the Ionic columns of the original building, carved out of single oak trunks, still separate the aisle from the nave. While it retains these typical late seventeenth-century features, the building has a strong contemporary feel. This is achieved by the clear glazing, from 1959, white walls and dramatic early twenty-first-century reordering to allow for worship around an altar centrally placed in the nave.

ABOVE: Organ case in the north aisle of the church, made for the Duke of Chandos by Abraham Jordan in 1720,

The church's rich music programme, with regular concerts, owes much to its historic organ, originally from the Duke of Chandos's estate in Edgware, where George Frideric Handel was the director of music. Handel would have played the instrument, which, extensively rebuilt, now sits to the north of the chancel.

Although a twentieth-century block of flats sadly now impedes the waterfront view, the church makes a delightful excursion by four-minute passenger ferry from Portsmouth (ferries run approximately every ten minutes); looking back, you can glimpse the lantern of Portsmouth Cathedral.

*Hawksmoor's first church under the Fifty New Churches Act, 1711*

# St Alfege, Greenwich (Diocese of Southwark)

Nicholas Hawksmoor, 1712–14

See website for opening times
www.st-alfege.org  🐦 @StAlfegeChurch
Postcode: SE10 9BJ

REPUTEDLY ON THE SITE of the martyrdom of Alfege, Archbishop of Canterbury, by Vikings in 1012, the medieval church was rebuilt by Nicholas Hawksmoor under the Fifty New Churches Act of 1711. Rich in history, it is the burial place of Thomas Tallis and James Wolfe.

Hawksmoor's design, based on the classical temple or basilica structure, was intended to suggest a return to early Christianity after the religious turmoil in England of the previous 200 years. A grassed courtyard to the west end continues the temple plan.

Facing the busy road, the Doric east portico, with its simple Greek-style Tuscan columns, has a hint of the baroque in its broken pediment and four drum-shaped 'altars' decorated with infant angels. Apparently the unfilled niche behind the broken pediment was intended for a statue of Queen Anne.

The biggest single unsupported roof of its time spans a spacious and broad interior. Hawksmoor was able to employ the very best and – thanks to Greenwich royal palace and Deptford dockyards nearby – local craftsmen, including Grinling Gibbons for the woodwork, Jean Tijou for the altar screen and Sir James Thornhill for the *trompe l'œil* painting behind the altar.

Most church communities would be very envious of the four enclosed eighteenth-century meeting rooms. However, money ran out for the tower, which was only completed 30 years later by John James, who re-faced the medieval tower. It has 10 bells.

St Alfege's hosts free concerts and runs numerous activities to support the community, including a winter night shelter and supper club. The church is embarking on a Heritage Lottery Fund project, which will include improving the landscaping and access around this prominent building.

ABOVE: A delightful extravagance to have four staircases, all finished with fine wood Corinthian columns and capitals carved by Grinling Gibbons.

OPPOSITE: Built in brick and faced with Portland stone, the east end exterior was recently cleaned and conserved, thanks to local fundraising and a landfill tax grant.

*Palladian church with trompe l'œil painted interior*

# St Lawrence, Mereworth (Diocese of Rochester)

Constructed 1744–6

Open daily
www.kmwchurches.org/mereworth
Postcode: ME18 5LY

The eighteenth-century Grand Tour, which educated gentlemen in all things classical, and the Palladian style had less impact on churches than on country-house building. St Lawrence's Church is a rare exception. John Fane, 7th Earl of Westmorland, demolished Mereworth's medieval church for architect and author Colen Campbell (*Vitruvius Britannicus*, 1715) to build Mereworth Castle explicitly in imitation of Palladio's Villa Rotunda in Vicenza. Campbell had died by the time the church was rebuilt and its architect is not documented, but was most likely Campbell's pupil, Roger Morris.

The church is a rectangular single-storey box with a pitched roof and overhanging eaves (like Inigo Jones's St Paul's, Covent Garden) and a semicircular portico at the west end (see front cover). Externally what is most striking is the very tall, four-tier steeple rising up through the roof in the style of St Martin-in-the-Fields in London. In 2008 new urns were introduced on the eight angles of the lantern.

Inside, the nave is three times as long as it is wide, the feeling of space emphasised by the lack of a separate chancel, and is dominated by baseless Roman Doric columns. The barrel-vaulted roof frames the east-end Diocletian (semicircular) window and all the surfaces are painted with *trompe l'œil* architectural effects, a special glory of the church, including painted swags, crossed palm trophies and symbols of the Father, Son and Holy Spirit on the frieze.

The painted decoration has recently been conserved. The church is maintained by, amongst others, a highly knowledgeable descendant of the Fane family.

ABOVE: Large flower head encircled by mouldings painted on the aisle ceilings.

OPPOSITE: *Trompe l'œil* painted coffering on the ceiling, above a painted organ over the west end gallery, where musicians would have played before it was customary for choirs to sing at the east end.

*Rural church with splendid Italianate baroque decoration verging on rococo*

# St Michael and All Angels, Great Witley (Diocese of Worcester)

Possibly by James Gibbs, early eighteenth century

See website for opening times
www.greatwitleychurch.org.uk
Postcode: WR6 6JT

ST MICHAEL'S, a classical rectangular box with pedimented porch and cupola-topped square tower, was commissioned by Lord and Lady Foley of Witley Court to replace an earlier church and was consecrated in 1735. Inside is the Foley funerary monument by the Flemish sculptor John Rysbrack. With seven larger than life-sized figures, this must be one of the largest monuments in an English parish church.

Apart from the gilded cupola, nothing from the outside prepares you for the Italianate Baroque splendour contained within. Here, in a grand recycling scheme, following the auction in 1747 of the Duke of Chandos's palace and chapel at Cannons in Middlesex,

we find ceiling paintings by Antonio Bellucci, enamel painted windows and a splendid organ, all set within the most gorgeous gilded decoration. It seems to be of stucco but the craftsmen made use of the newly invented papier mâché instead, presumably to reduce weight. It is incredible how this ensemble, made for another chapel around 1720, fits so perfectly at Great Witley. Each element is astonishing, not least the pictorial window scheme of biblical scenes made by Joshua Price after designs by Francisco Slater.

The visitor approaches either from Great Witley village via a long and untarmacked drive or by visiting adjacent Witley Court, tragically damaged by fire in 1937 and now managed by English Heritage. Although the house was abandoned by its aristocratic owner, the church remained the parish church of Great Witley and it is impressive the way parishioners and local people have taken on the care and ongoing conservation of the church. Volunteers man the church daily and they have opened up the crypt, still containing eighteenth-century coffins. A local couple set up a tearoom nearby to refresh the intrepid visitor. This is now owned by the church and offers a warm welcome and delicious cakes!

*Fanciful and celebratory Strawberry Hill Gothick set piece*

# St John the Evangelist, Shobdon (Diocese of Hereford)

Built on the site of an earlier Norman church, 1749–56

Open daily until dusk, or later by arrangement
www.shobdonchurch.org.uk
Postcode: HR6 9LZ (nearer to Shobdon Village: follow signs in order to avoid a private drive and barrier)

THE OGEE-HOODED DOORWAY and cusping on the west tower entrance are hints of what is to come, but nothing prepares you for the icing-sugar confection of Strawberry Hill Gothick inside St John, Shobdon. In place of dark oak, the whole church is painted white with pale Wedgwood-blue detailing in a joyful and eccentric design of wavy ogees and cusped pew ends.

Viscount Bateman knew of Horace Walpole's very personal and fanciful house at Strawberry Hill, Twickenham, and wanted something like it – in the middle of rural Herefordshire. His uncle, a friend of Horace Walpole, was well placed to supervise the project for him. Broadly described as English Rococo, its detailing is a wild mix of Gothic, Chinoiserie and Arab in inspiration.

The Bateman family had a comfortable family 'pew', complete with Gothick fireplace, in the south transept. More like a little sitting room, it's easy to imagine them sitting here and enjoying the sight of their creation – as well as listening to the sermon.

Most of the original Georgian glass survives. In the nave, stylised flowers in bright primary yellows, blues and reds punctuate the otherwise clear glass, and streams of coloured light play over the white of the interior.

A painted stage-set like this needs constant attention. Remarkably, the small but energetic local community recently raised over £1.25 million to repair the roof and plasterwork to maintain this glorious and very English eighteenth-century celebration of life.

The original Norman font is still inside; the arches from the earlier church were re-erected at the end of a tree-lined avenue in the manner of an eighteenth-century folly when the church was rebuilt.

OPPOSITE: The *pièce de résistance* of the Strawberry Hill Gothick interior: a glorious triple-decker pulpit topped with a pierced crown made of volutes and crocketed pinnacles.

*Georgian 'preaching box' in a medieval church*

## St Edith of Polesworth, Orton-on-the-Hill (Diocese of Leicester)

Early fourteenth century, with interior furnishings of 1764

Regularly open on Saturdays and Sundays, April to October, and by arrangement at other times

www.achurchnearyou.com/orton-on-the-hill-st-edith-of-polesworth

Postcode: CV9 3NG

FROM THE OUTSIDE St Edith's is an imposing stone church, primarily of the fourteenth century. Enter, and one steps into the eighteenth century.

The church offers a good lesson in how church interiors were altered to suit worship in the centuries between the English Reformation and the Victorian revival of ritualism. The focus of worship was preaching, so the interior is dominated by a substantial 'triple-decker' pulpit. The sermon was given from the top level; the lesson was read from the middle; and the clerk, who led the responses of the congregation, sat at the bottom. The pulpit was placed on the north wall so as to be visible to as many people as possible across the nave and aisle.

Simple medieval bench seating (a couple of examples remain in the south porch) was replaced by high-sided 'box pews', each with its own door. With the church effectively reorientated towards the north, the altar at the east end was literally sidelined. The church also retains, in the south aisle, its Georgian 'baluster' font, which bears a large inscription recording the donor, S.S. Perkins Esq., and the date, 1764. Few complete Georgian church interiors of this kind now survive: the consensus among Victorian clergy and church builders, their views shaped by the influential Oxford Movement, was that box pews were socially divisive and that worship should be focused on ritual at the high altar.

OPPOSITE: Eighteenth-century triple-decker pulpit and box pews.

Part of a large multi-parish rural benefice, St Edith's is well loved by its local community. Popular events held in the church include concerts, harvest suppers and bell-ringing.

*Typical neoclassical church with distinguished eighteenth century east window*

## St Paul, Birmingham (Diocese of Birmingham)

Built as part of the city's Georgian suburban development, 1777–9

Open Tuesday to Saturday 10am to 4pm
www.stpaulsjq.church
Postcode: B3 1QZ

THE CHURCH OF St Paul is an important remnant of Birmingham's history: part of the Georgian expansion of the city, subsequently surrounded by the workshops of the Jewellery Quarter, now at the heart of one of the most thriving and transformed areas of the capital of the Midlands. The building acts as a performance venue for community theatre and concerts, and is open throughout the week for drop-in visitors.

Planned as the centrepiece of a formal residential square – a quintessentially eighteenth-century urban development – the church was erected between 1777 and 1779 to a design by master joiner and architect Roger Eykyn, with the spire added 40 years later. The church is not on a traditional east-west axis but instead follows the regimented grid of the surrounding streets.

In many respects St Paul's is a typical Georgian church, with cues taken from James Gibbs and clear echoes of St Martin-in-the-Fields, London. It is neoclassical in style, its simple 'box' form set out with galleries and numbered box pews. Particularly appealing are the upholstered pews in coved recesses to either side of the west door.

However, the feature that truly marks out St Paul's is the east window. Showing the conversion of Paul, this was executed in 1791 by local artist Francis Eginton, following a design by Benjamin West, the celebrated Anglo-American painter of epic historical scenes. The window is painted on the inner and outer surfaces of a double thickness of glazing – a technique revived in the Georgian period. The colours are deep and dark, the scene one of confusion and desperation; but with the morning light streaming through, the figures emerge, glowing, from the brooding storm.

ABOVE: Detail from the east window by Francis Eginton, 1791, of the Conversion of St Paul.

*Urban church showing both Georgian and Gothic influences*

## St George, Chorley (Diocese of Blackburn)

Commissioners' church by Thomas Rickman, 1822–5,
modified 1890s and 1950s

Open on Wednesday and Sunday mornings, and by arrangement at other times

www.stgeorgechorley.co.uk

Postcode: PR7 2AA

ST GEORGE'S CHURCH perfectly illustrates the economic, social and intellectual preoccupations of its time. It was one of the Commissioners' churches, part of a surge in church-building during the first half of the nineteenth century encouraged by a government concerned that the industrial revolution was creating urban areas bereft of the influence of the Church. Designed by Thomas Rickman, the essentially Georgian plan is enlivened with Gothic detailing and innovative use of ironwork.

Capacity was all-important for the new Commissioners' churches: St George's, a large rectangular space with galleries on three sides, was designed to hold over 2,000 people. Pews and benches occupied every available inch and a reading desk stood centrally in front of the altar so that all could see and hear the minister deliver the Word.

Chorley is more than a preaching box, though: the Commissioners favoured the Gothic style, and Rickman, famous for classifying medieval architecture, incorporated paired lancet windows in the Early English style as well as external buttresses with pinnacles and unusual chamfers, and a crocketed gable over the west doorway.

Inside is a wealth of decorative detail: the galleries, which have their original pews, have traceried fronts and are supported by slender columns with attached shafts. The cast iron hammerbeams supporting the flat ceiling have sexfoil spandrels.

When the organ was moved from the west end in 1891, Stephen Adam designed a fine stained-glass window to fill the gap in the tower arch. Protected from the elements, its Pre-Raphaelite figures are still wonderfully crisp and can be viewed up close from the ringing chamber. While there, it is worth noting the unusual Ellacombe chimes.

This is a much-loved church and the parish has recently secured funding from the Heritage Lottery Fund to carry out urgent repairs.

ABOVE: Detail of the west end window showing the Resurrection in the Pre-Raphaelite style by Stephen Adam, 1891.

OPPOSITE: Baptism at Thomas Rickman's preaching box for the industrial age (with later modifications).

*Parish church that houses a meeting of the national parliament*

## St John the Baptist (Diocese of Sodor and Man)

Richard Lane of Manchester, 1849

Open daily 9am to 6pm
www.achurchnearyou.com/tynwaldchurch
Postcode: IM4 3NA

St John's stands on the site of an ancient keeill, a small Celtic chapel. The base of an ancient cross inscribed 'but Osruth carved these Runes' was found after the demolition of the previous church.

St John's was one of the first churches on the Isle of Man to reflect the Ecclesiological movement for worship centred on the high altar with the priest facing east. Elements of this layout remain, although the arrangements in the sanctuary have seen the English altar, its riddle posts and curtains still in place, moved forward to allow the minister to face the congregation while celebrating communion.

Although it is the parish church, St John's has other roles, as a national church for the island and as a meeting place for the court of Tynwald, the island's parliament. A service is held here each Tynwald Day (5 July) to begin the day's proceedings. Everyone then processes out of the west door to Tynwald Hill, where the laws are announced in Manx and English. At the end of the day the members return to the church for the laws to be signed.

In the crossing are seats for members of the lower chamber of Tynwald, the House of Keys; members of the upper chamber, the Legislative Council, sit in the chancel. There is a plaque on every seat indicating where each office-holder is to sit.

The church contains a series of stained-glass windows illustrating the Annunciation, Crucifixion, Resurrection and the saints of the ancient island parish churches. It is open daily.

ABOVE: Tynwald seating in the nave.

OPPOSITE: Tynwald Day ceremony 2016.

*Vibrant Victorian visual inventiveness*

## St Peter, Hascombe (Diocese of Guildford)

Henry Woodyer, 1864

Open daily 8am to 6pm

www.achurchnearyou.com/hascombe-st-peter

Postcode: GU8 4JD

FOR SHEER VISUAL DELIGHT the finest Victorian churches can rival the best buildings of any date in this country. The churches of Henry Woodyer are exemplary, displaying an imaginative handling of vernacular forms and, frequently, internal decoration of breathtaking richness and kaleidoscopic vibrancy of colour.

St Peter's at Hascombe is one of Woodyer's loveliest. The exterior, Early English in style with some quirky details such as an east window pierced through a buttress, is charming and characterful, but the interior is unforgettable. Inside, every surface is covered in colour and pattern, from the nave walls, on which glittering fish leap in golden nets (St Peter was, of course, a fisherman), to the rood screen on which each roll of the moulding bears a different motif. It culminates in an astonishing chancel (see also image on back cover).

Though Hascombe is a small village, worship is held in the church every Sunday. Every saint's day is kept and the church is popular for weddings and concerts.

Nearby is Woodyer's own church, St Andrew at Grafham. Woodyer built it as a memorial to his wife, whose jewels were used to ornament the communion vessels. Its interior once rivalled Hascombe's, but the walls were whitewashed in the 1950s; however, it still boasts a brightly decorated chancel ceiling and rood screen, and a superb floor-to-ceiling reredos depicting a great vine, springing from the cross, in which angels sit like singing birds. Woodyer is buried in the churchyard. St Michael and all Angels, Waterford, in the St Albans diocese (page 76), was also designed by Henry Woodyer.

ABOVE: Exterior designed in the Early English style.

OPPOSITE: Medieval rood screen painted in the nineteenth-century chancel, with a gilded ceiling formed of deep ribs, like an upturned boat, and a reredos thronged with saints and angels whose golden haloes glitter in the candlelight.

*Church rebuilt to adorn a great estate*

## St Peter, Edensor, Chatsworth Estate (Diocese of Derby)

Medieval, rebuilt by Sir George Gilbert Scott, 1867

Open daily 9am to 5pm (or dusk, if earlier)
www.stpetersedensor.org
Postcode: DE45 1PH

EVERY PARISH CHURCH tells a story about the community that built and shaped it. In the case of St Peter's church at Edensor (pronounced 'Ensor') in Derbyshire, it is the story of a family and its house: the Cavendishes, Dukes of Devonshire, and Chatsworth.

Edensor once lay on the River Derwent, below Chatsworth. The 6th Duke wished the village to be out of sight of the house, however, so between 1838 and 1842 it was moved to its present site. The most successful architect of his day, Sir George Gilbert Scott, was chosen for the new church. He designed the church in the Early English style, incorporating fragments of the previous Norman church in the south porch. Everything inside is of the highest quality, without flamboyance: witness the rich alabaster and marbles of the pulpit, the patterned stone floor, the fine oak furnishings and the sedilia adorned with delicately carved ferns.

The church features many memorials to the Cavendishes. The less ostentatious Cavendish family plot can be found at the far end of the tussocky, sheep-grazed churchyard. Also buried at Edensor is Sir Joseph Paxton, architect of the Crystal Palace, who began his career as a gardener's boy on the Chatsworth estate.

As well as serving the local community, St Peter's welcomes many tourists visiting Chatsworth House and its estate.

OPPOSITE: The gigantic monument to Henry and William Cavendish (died 1616 and 1625 respectively). They lie under a black marble canopy, Henry shown as a skeleton and William in his winding-sheet, while above them hang robes and armour and an angel trumpeting their achievements.

*High Victorian jewel-box*

## St John, Tuebrook (Diocese of Liverpool)

George Frederick Bodley, 1867–70

Open Tuesday and Saturday 9.30 to noon, and by arrangement at other times
www.stjohntuebrook.net  ✹@StJohnTuebrook
Postcode: L13 7EA

JUST AS THE WEALTH of medieval Norfolk is displayed in that diocese's fourteenth- and fifteenth-century churches, so the power and glory of nineteenth-century Liverpool remains apparent in the unparalleled splendour of its Victorian places of worship. From the extraordinary 'iron church' of St George, Everton, to G.E. Street's glittering St Margaret of Antioch in Toxteth and J.L. Pearson's majestic St Agnes in Sefton Park – along with Liverpool's Roman Catholic, Greek Orthodox and Jewish sacred buildings – the city showcases the best of nineteenth-century religious architecture.

One of the finest examples is the church of St John the Baptist at Tuebrook, in the north-east of the city. It was designed by G.F. Bodley, the leading architect of the later Gothic Revival in England (and, at the very end of his career, designer of the Washington National Cathedral in the USA). Exemplifying the generous philanthropy of the age, the building's entire cost was covered by a single donor and no expense was spared.

The breathtaking interior of St John's church puts all of Bodley's supreme decorative inventiveness on display. Every surface sings with colour and pattern. Stencilled decorations cover the walls and ceiling, and even the roof beams are painted with hymn lyrics. The magnificent rood screen, glittering with gold leaf, gives on to a glorious chancel. Fine works by other artists complement Bodley's achievement, including stained glass by Morris & Co., a mural of the Tree of Life about the chancel arch by C.E. Kempe and a statue of John the Baptist by J.N. Comper, given as a Second World War memorial. Every element of the building is in harmony.

The present congregation brings its own harmony to the church, with a regular choir and organist leading a choral Anglo-Catholic liturgy.

OPPOSITE: Close up of the rood screen, also showing colours and patterns of many other decorated surfaces, including the organ.

*Rochdale's temple to freemasonry*

# St Edmund, Falinge, Rochdale (Diocese of Manchester)

James Medland and Henry Taylor 1870

See website for opening times
www.visitchurches.org.uk/Ourchurches/Completelistofchurches/Church-of-St-Edmund-Falinge-Greater-Manchester
Postcode: OL12 6QF

SAINT EDMUND'S CHURCH, Falinge, has been in the care of the Churches Conservation Trust since 2012. The church is an extraordinary example of masonic architecture commissioned by local industrialist and Freemason Albert Hudson Royds. It is the only known church building of its type in England and is lavishly embellished with rich ornamentation and masonic symbolism such as set squares, triangles and pairs of compasses.

The quality of the art and craftsmanship is of an extremely high standard, endorsed by the Victorian Society, which described St Edmund's as 'unusual and extraordinary'. Nikolaus Pevsner described the building as 'Rochdale's temple to Freemasonry, a total concept as exotic as Rosslyn Chapel in Scotland'. The church was built at the highest point in the town and set in a diamond-shaped churchyard, thus making an overt reference to the Temple that dominated Jerusalem.

As part of St Edmund's rescue, the Churches Conservation Trust has invested in three recent phases of conservation and repair, restoring the church to its former glory.

St Edmund's is now managed locally by a team of dedicated volunteers who open the church for visitors and tour groups, and run a calendar of cultural events including contemporary art installations. The church has also been used by the local primary school to teach religious education in what is now a largely multicultural community; its future is more secure than it was in 2007, when the church closed to regular worship. The local community continues to care for the church and is proud to share it with visitors and show them the building's many secrets.

OPPOSITE: Lectern incorporating builders' tools and masonic symbolism.

# St Michael and All Angels, Waterford (Diocese of St Albans)

Henry Woodyer, 1872

Open every Wednesday afternoon and by request to the churchwarden
www.achurchnearyou.com/waterford-st-michael-all-angels
Postcode: SG14 2PS

MODEST WATERFORD CHURCH was built by nineteenth-century lord of the manor and banker Robert Smith. He commissioned renowned architect Henry Woodyer (St Peter's, Hascombe, page 69), who deployed avant-garde artists and the best materials available to decorate the church.

On entering, one is immediately impressed by the architectural font cover, a highly skilled piece of carpentry with a pulley for raising and lowering. The visitor's eye is then drawn to the colourful mosaics and tiles of the chancel, with its gilded reredos by Powell & Sons. It is only then that one begins to appreciate the stained glass in every window, particularly those created by Morris & Co.

The east window features a Nativity scene by Sir Edward Burne-Jones, surrounded by four musical angels designed by William Morris himself. Above these are quatrefoils containing angel faces, possibly by Dante Gabriel Rossetti, one of which is an image of Morris's wife, Jane.

The West End, near the font, has three windows with a watery theme: St Philip the Deacon, with water shown flowing over his feet, and Noah, both by Ford Madox Brown, and John the Baptist by Burne-Jones.

One can get up close to Burne-Jones's three-light window of angels gazing at the ascended Christ and see the texture of the glass (opposite). Most striking is his Dance of Celebration by the Prophetess Miriam in the chancel. White-robed Miriam, full-length and in profile, is enraptured, her snake-like hair flying, against a gorgeous background of foliage and pomegranates. Burne-Jones's Greek muse, Maria Zambaco, is clearly the model for Miriam (right).

VIRI GAL
ILAEI QVID
STATIS AS
PICIENTES
IN COELV
HIC IESVS
QVI ASSVM
PTVS EST A

VOBIS IN
COELVM SIC
VENIET QVE
MADMODVM
VIDISTIS
EVNTEM
IN COELV

*Centre of Anglican worship in Rome, 'might not be out of place in Maida Vale or Manchester'*

## All Saints Anglican Church, Rome (Diocese of Europe)

George Edmund Street, 1882–1885

Church office open Monday to Friday 9am to 3pm
www.allsaintsrome.org  🐦@Allsaintsrome
Via del Babuino, 153, 00187 Rome, Italy

ANGLICAN WORSHIP in Rome began 200 years ago, when the Reverend Corbert Hue began to take services for English residents in his lodgings near the Spanish Steps. The congregation quickly established itself and found its first permanent home on the first floor of a building near the Porta del Popolo. Although the church flourished, this accommodation was not ideal – for one thing, the ground floor was occupied by a tavern known for its wild beast shows – so in 1872 the members of the congregation approached George Edmund Street to design a new place of worship for them.

Street was one of the leading architects of the Victorian Gothic revival. Perhaps best known for the Law Courts in the Strand in London, he was a prolific builder of churches in England and internationally; in Rome he also designed the Episcopal church of St Paul's Within the Walls, famous for its mosaic decorations by Edward Burne-Jones. He was a pioneer in the use of 'constructional polychromy' in architecture, whereby decoration is not applied to surfaces but rather built into a structure through the use of differently coloured materials, as seen in All Saints' use of red brick and stone for the walls and coloured marbles for the nave columns.

All Saints was Street's last commission; he did not live to see the laying of the foundation stone in 1882. The church opened for worship on Easter Day in 1887, though its prominent white spire was not finished until 1937. Aside from a brief hiatus during the Second World War, it has remained the focus of worship and social life for Anglicans in Rome ever since, and it is equally renowned as a centre for music and for ecumenical engagement in the city.

ABOVE: St George, patron saint of England, and the slain dragon.

OPPOSITE: An English church spire in the Roman roofscape.

*A church shaped by Empire*

## St Andrew and St Patrick, Elveden (Diocese of St Edmundsbury and Ipswich)

Medieval, restored by John Norton, 1869; enlarged 1904–6 and 1922 by W.D. Caröe

Open Wednesdays 10.30am to 3pm in June, July and August and by arrangement at other times (01842 890540)
www.achurchnearyou.com/elveden-st-andrew-st-patrick
Postcode: IP24 3TQ

St Andrew and St Patrick at Elveden, like St Peter's church at Edensor (see page 70), is an estate church, serving the neighbouring Elveden Hall. Whereas Edensor reflects the history of one of the oldest-established families of the English aristocracy, however, Elveden was shaped by two figures who began their lives at the edges of the British Empire.

The first was Duleep Singh, last of the Sikh maharajahs. He came to the throne at the age of five, in 1843, but was deposed aged ten when the British annexed the Punjab. He converted to Christianity and was sent into exile in Britain. He purchased the Elveden estate in 1863 and had its medieval flint church, dedicated to St Andrew, restored.

Of the present church, the medieval building restored by Singh forms merely the south aisle and chapel. In 1894 the estate was bought by Edward Guinness (of the Irish brewing dynasty), later first Earl of Iveagh, who added the dedication to St Patrick and commissioned W.D. Caröe to enlarge the church. Caröe decorated the interior, with sumptuous richness, in a style that has been termed 'Art Nouveau Gothic': the result is extraordinary. The church is thronged with exquisite wood-carving and stonework, an alabaster reredos fills the entire east wall, and even the floor tiles are ornamented with emblems of the British nations. The beautiful bell tower and cloister to the south were built in memory of Lady Iveagh in 1922.

Though the days of the great houses have passed, the Elveden estate continues to thrive and St Andrew and St Patrick still serves its community as the parish church.

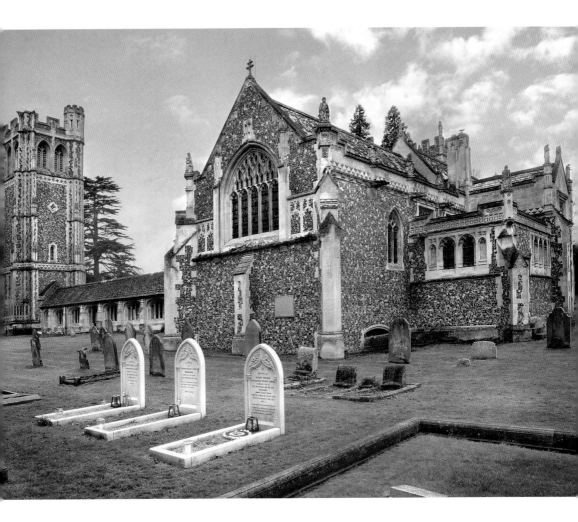

ABOVE: Maharajah Duleep Singh re-converted to Sikhism before his death in Paris in 1893 and is buried beside his wife and son in the churchyard at Elveden. The church welcomes many Sikh visitors. The tower is connected to the church by a cloister, a grand entrance for the landowners next door.

*The Arts and Crafts cathedral of the north-east*

## St Andrew, Roker, Monkwearmouth (Diocese of Durham)

Edward Shroeder Prior and Albert Randall Wells, 1907

Open weekdays 9am to 1pm
www.monkwearmouthcofe.com/st.-andrew-s.html
Postcode: SR6 9PT

THE BENEFACTOR JOHN PRIESTMAN, a local shipbuilder, built St Andrew's as a memorial to his mother on a grand scale. He enlisted the talents of some of the leading architects of the Arts and Crafts movement: Edward Schroeder trained under Richard Norman Shaw and A. Randall Wells, commissioned to assist him, was an associate of William Lethaby.

The imposing stone church stands within an Edwardian suburb, now a conservation area. Of overall familiar ecclesiastical form, it is composed of quirky, irregular Gothic motifs.

An unobstructed view up the wide nave is made possible by the great spans of reinforced concrete arches that make up the roof. Combined with timber, it resembles the keel of a boat. Unplastered stone walls create a cave-like space, with light seeping in through hand-made rippled glazing, like the shimmering surface of the sea nearby.

In contrast to the simplicity of the nave, the chancel is polychrome and splendid, adorned with works by leading Arts and Crafts artists. A William Morris carpet installed in 1907, a tapestry of the Presentation of the Three Kings by Sir Edward Burne-Jones and stained glass by H.A. Payne are topped by an unusual mural of the Creation by MacDonald Gill (brother of Eric), which uses an electric light for the sun!

Unfortunately the friable limestone walls cause maintenance issues, hence the church features on Historic England's Heritage at Risk register. The Heritage Lottery Fund and others, including the National Churches Trust, have funded window repairs; other works, including access improvements, remain outstanding.

ABOVE: The William Morris carpet in the chancel was recently conserved with support from the Church Buildings Council's '100 Church Treasures' campaign and the Andrew Lloyd Webber Foundation. Plans are afoot to conserve Burne-Jones's spectacular tapestry that hangs over the altar.

*Italianate brick and concrete mission church*

# St Barnabas, Dalston (Diocese of London)

Sir Charles Reilly, 1910

Usually open daily; tucked away, this hidden gem would benefit from better signage and additional opening hours
www.saintbarnabasdalston.org.uk  ✈ @StBarnysDalston
Postcode: E8 2EA

IN THE TRADITION of English public schools, both St Barnabas and the mission building that entirely hides it from view were built to provide for the poor of East London – in this case by the Merchant Taylors' School. It was a former student at the school who built the church some two decades after he had visited the mission.

Charles Reilly designed many buildings but built surprisingly few; nevertheless, he is acknowledged to be a major figure in the history of British architecture, thanks to the influence he wielded as Director of the Liverpool School of Architecture. Although Britain's modest Byzantine revival had almost run its course by the start of the twentieth century (Westminster Cathedral being a notable exception), it seems to have provided Reilly with the inspiration for St Barnabas with its round arches, vaulted nave and domed chancel.

Unlike Westminster Cathedral, St Barnabas is almost completely lacking in adornment, although Reilly had always intended a chancel screen; this was finally installed in 1935, largely by Herbert Tyson Smith. The colourful paintwork and intricate detailing of the metalwork are in striking contrast to the rest of the interior, which is industrial in its starkness and volume, and seen by some as heralding the modernist movement. Reilly considered it his best work.

St Barnabas was closed for many years so it is good to see that it now has a new lease of life, thanks to a team from a sister church in Hackney, and ministers to the local artists, families and community. The mission hall has been sensitively adapted for modern use and plays host to a wide range of activities, from community choir to life drawing.

ABOVE: Cross and candlesticks by Liverpool sculptor Herbert Tyson Smith.

OPPOSITE: Tyson Smith's painted and gilded screen, added in 1935, divides the monumental unadorned chancel and nave.

*Temple Moore's finest Edwardian Gothic Revival church*

# St Wilfrid, Harrogate (Diocese of Leeds)

Temple Moore and his son-in-law Leslie Moore, 1904–35

Open 7.30am to 6.45pm
www.stwilfrid.org
Postcode: HG1 2EY

ST WILFRID'S CHURCH left such an impression on Sir John Betjeman that it found its way into one of his poems ('O, I wad gang tae Harrogate tae a kirk by Temple Moore, Wi' a tall choir and a lang nave and rush mats on the floor'). Architect Sir Aston Webb described it as 'perhaps the most beautiful of all parish churches I know'.

A church had been planned to serve the growing spa town of Harrogate, but it was chance tragedy that led to one of such grandeur: it was built largely on bequests by Jean Trotter, whose sister died unexpectedly here en route from London to Edinburgh in 1902.

Work began in 1904 to designs by Temple Moore, one of the most significant church architects of the Edwardian period. The first phase (nave, crossing and chancel) was completed by June 1914, when the church was consecrated. Following Moore's death in 1920, his son-in-law Leslie Moore carried on to complete his vision.

ABOVE: The church, in a residential area of Harrogate, gives the impression of a medieval French monastery.

OPPOSITE: The east end and chancel, with a view through to the lower-level Lady Chapel.

Approaching from the south, St Wilfrid's appears as a squat but vast church in a robust Early English style that suggests a rural medieval monastery. Upon entering, the visitor is first struck by the lofty nave, before turning east to see the progression of spaces, with plays of light and shadow, as the lower-level Lady Chapel is glimpsed through arched openings behind the altar. The minimal embellishments are offset by splashes of colour in the expressive rood, the traditional saints' figures on the pulpit and the richly coloured stained glass.

St Wilfrid's runs a packed programme of services throughout the week and provides an important facility for a wide range of local community groups.

*Fourteenth-century church with notable twentieth-century mural*

# St Martin of Tours, Bilborough, Nottingham (Diocese of Southwell and Nottingham)

1350–1450, restored 1877–8, extended 1972

Open Wednesday 10am to 4pm, Friday and Saturday 11am to 3pm, and by arrangement at other times
www.stmartinshiddentreasures.org.uk  💬@StMartinsBilb

Postcode: NG8 3BH

NOT ONLY IS THIS church now hidden within a modern Nottingham housing estate, it is further concealed by a vast and unforgiving flat-roofed 1970s windowless brick extension. Nestled at the core is a small red sandstone nave, chancel and west tower dating from 1350–1450 and restored in the nineteenth century. Hidden inside, rewarding both visitor and worshipper alike, is a recently conserved twentieth-century mural painting.

The Annunciation was painted in 1946 in an Italian Renaissance style and is a rare surviving monumental work by the female war artist Evelyn Gibbs, with the assistance of Claude Price. Gibbs, better known for her illustrations and etchings, had moved to Nottinghamshire at the outbreak of the Second World War with Goldsmiths College, where she was teaching.

Composed of two figures, St Mary to the left of the window and the Angel Gabriel to the right, the mural, with its background scenes of local Wollaton Hall and farm buildings, gives a sense of the church's former agricultural setting. The paintings have only recently been revealed, having been hidden for 42 years by a suspended ceiling and modern emulsion paint. The restoration project also saw the building reordered, including installation of new lighting and heating (from a ground source heat pump), and made accessible and reopened to the community.

Nineteenth-century plumbers' and lovers' hand and footmarks, found imprinted in the lead roof covering, are also displayed at the bottom of the tower. Their volume and range of styles and designs of footwear, suggests that the church was popular with tourists of the time.

OPPOSITE: The award-winning project to reveal Evelyn Gibbs's Annunciation is part of a wider and ongoing renewal of the church.

The church also contains the remains of a tomb to Edmund Helwys of Broxtowe Hall. His son, Thomas, was married in the church and became the co-founder of the Baptist denomination.

*Bold modern church, born out of Second World War destruction*

## St Mark, Broomhill, Sheffield (Diocese of Sheffield)

George Pace, 1961–3, incorporating tower of 1868–71

Open Monday to Friday 8.30 to 5.30pm
www.stmarkssheffield.co.uk
Postcode: S10 2SE

ON THE NIGHT of 12 December 1940 St Mark's Church, on one of Sheffield's seven hills, received a direct hit by a Luftwaffe bomb. Of the Victorian building only the external walls and the west tower were left standing. The parish enlisted George Pace, one of the twentieth century's most distinguished church architects, to rebuild its church. The first design was produced in 1950 but it was not until 1961 that work began. The tower – a typical Gothic Revival work by W.H. Crossland – would be retained, but the new body of the church would be distinctly modern.

The church reflected architecturally the changes towards a new and radical style of worship that St Mark's embraced in the 1960s. Rather than reinstating a traditional cruciform plan, the church is a distorted, open-plan hexagon. The altar is simply raised on a low dais at the east end; the font is set on the northern side of the nave.

The simplicity of the building's interior provides a backdrop for its fantastic stained-glass windows. The Te Deum window to the east, set within robust concrete tracery forming an abstract Tree of Jesse, is by Harry Stammers: the Trinity forms the central part of the window, surrounded by expressive figures moving in and out of frame. To the west is a mesmerising Pentecostal window of abstract flames in glowing colours designed by John Piper and Patrick Reyntiens.

St Mark's today proudly continues to provide a base for the radical theology and inclusive ministry and outreach that the building was built to express.

ABOVE: George Pace's post-war nave. Energy is now provided by solar panels on the roof.

OPPOSITE: Harry Stammers's Te Deum window at the east end of Pace's nave, depicting the Trinity, many saints and naturalistic details, including a mouse and a spider's web.

*Prizewinning contemporary elliptical chapel likened to a floating ship*

## Bishop Edward King Chapel, Ripon College, Cuddesdon (Diocese of Oxford)

Architect Niall McLaughlin, completed 2013

Visitors welcome on weekdays, by arrangement (01865 874404)
www.rcc.ac.uk/chapel
Postcode: OX44 9EX

DEDICATED TO Bishop Edward King, the chapel of this theological training college is also home to a small community of sisters and is set apart from other buildings in a beautiful natural site overlooking open countryside. Elliptical in plan, it is built of Clipsham ashlar stone with high-level windows providing natural light (see image below).

Collegiate in design, the worship space uses curved benches with two un-hierarchical focal points, the altar and lectern. A small devotional side chapel leads off for the community of nuns, and angled ground-level windows let in light whilst maintaining the privacy of the worship space. Natural light and efficient use of energy were part of the building's brief.

Calm and lofty, the building doesn't seek to impose and so is suited to personal devotion as well as communal worship, in which the acoustics allow a conversational rather than declaratory tone. The occasional sound of rustling leaves from outside adds to the otherworldliness of the chapel.

Its quiet architectural grandeur is perhaps lacking in some more functional modernist church buildings. At first appearance the chapel makes no allusion to tradition architectural styles, but the ship imagery and soaring heights of the single-storey building keep it rooted in the Christian ecclesiastical tradition. This ship of stone was inspired by Seamus Heaney's poem *Lightenings viii*, describing a ship floating into a monastery, and the sense of journey or pilgrimage seems very appropriate in a place of evolving vocations.

OPPOSITE: The interior is dominated by a tall, light-coloured timber structure and a lattice of vaulting floating apart from the ceiling, the whole resembling an upturned ship.

# ARCHITECTURAL STYLES

### Anglo-Saxon
Simple in its structure and detailing, but nonetheless retaining features derived from classical architecture such as the semicircular arch. Rubble masonry, sometimes incorporating older material such as Roman brick, is more likely to be met with than neatly squared stones. Window openings are small and often placed asymmetrically rather than conforming to an overall pattern.

### Norman
Originating in northern France and introduced to England on a wide scale following the Norman Conquest, it features massive round columns, thick stone walls and round arches, characteristically decorated with zigzag patterning and bold figural carving. It is also known as 'English Romanesque'. The cruciform church with a square crossing tower became common in this period.

### Medieval
'Gothic' architecture was introduced to England from France at the end of the twelfth century and would hold sway for the next 400 years. More than just a shift in styles, Gothic represented a revolution in engineering. It is characterised by pointed arches, soaring heights, thinner walls and more and larger windows, often containing colourful stained glass. In England the Gothic style developed in three phases:

*Early English*
The earliest phase of Gothic saw the introduction of pointed arches and narrow, pointed lancet windows: these enabled taller and lighter buildings to be constructed. Carved decoration was spare and typified by crisp, stylised foliage.

*Decorated*
Over time, window tracery became more elaborate and carved decoration more naturalistic, evolving into what is called the Decorated Style. This phase of Gothic also featured more slender columns and the use of decorative ribbed vaulting.

*Perpendicular*
Unique to England, the Perpendicular style featured strong grids of vertical and horizontal lines, huge window surfaces, and even more elaborate vaulting, culminating in the fan vault.

### Post-Reformation
The centuries following England's break from the Roman Church saw a return to architectural forms derived from classical and Renaissance architecture, in a plethora of styles from Jacobean to Baroque to Neoclassical. In the late eighteenth century there was a revival of interest in Gothic architecture for its romantic and literary associations, resulting in the fantastical style known as Strawberry Hill Gothick – the 'k' to distinguish it from medieval Gothic.

### Nineteenth century
A more scholarly return to Gothic was driven by a desire to recapture the spirit, as well as the outward forms, of medieval art and architecture. Numerous new churches and additions to existing churches were built in the Gothic style in England's expanding industrial towns and cities. The Arts and Crafts movement of the later nineteenth century opposed industrialisation and mass-production and promoted traditional craft skills: associated with William Morris and his followers, the movement was highly influential in the design of church furnishing and stained glass of the era.

### Twentieth and twenty-first centuries
Since the Second World War, architects have taken advantage of the structural possibilities of modern materials to give churches new and striking forms.

# GLOSSARY

**boss:** Decoratively carved block placed at the intersection of the ribs of a vault (q.v.).

**clerestory:** Upper storey of the nave rising above the aisle roofs, with windows to bring light to the central parts of a church.

**column:** Vertical structural element composed of a base, shaft and capital. Column capitals offer a simple means of differentiating the orders (or styles) of Classical architecture: Tuscan and Doric columns have plain capitals; Ionic capitals are characterised by coiled, scroll-like decorations; Corinthian capitals are ornamented with stylised acanthus leaves.

**corbel:** Block projecting from a wall to support a roof beam. Often decoratively carved.

**crocket:** Carved projection in the form of a bud, leaf or flower, in Gothic buildings often found, set at regular intervals, decorating the sides of gables, spires and pinnacles (q.v.).

**hammer-beam:** Type of roof-structure. Hammer-beams are short beams that do not span the entire width of a roof. They are supported on curved braces from the wall; resting on the hammer-beams are posts or arched braces which support the rafters. Hammer-beam roofs are often highly decorated, sometimes with carved angels.

**lancet:** Tall, narrow, pointed window openings. Found singly or in pairs in Early English Gothic buildings, or in larger groups in more complex Gothic tracery (q.v.).

**lantern:** Structure projecting from the roof of a building containing windows to light the interior; or a stage of a church tower that contains windows.

**misericord:** Projecting ledge on the underside of the hinged seat of a choir stall, on which clergy could perch when standing during long services – hence its name, meaning 'have pity.' Often richly decorated with carved foliage or allegorical figures.

**ogee:** An S-shaped curve, convex at top and concave at bottom.

**pilaster:** Representation in relief of a column (q.v.), projecting from the face of a wall.

**pinnacle:** Tall, thin, spire-like decorative feature, frequently used to crown a buttress. Often ornamented with crockets (q.v.).

**portico:** Porch with columns forming the entrance to a Classical building.

**reredos:** Carved or painted panel behind an altar.

**rood screen:** Decorated screen, topped with a cross, separating the chancel from the nave.

**sedilia:** Seats (usually three) on the south side of the chancel for officiating clergy. They are often recessed into the wall and may be decorated with elaborate canopies and pinnacles (q.v.).

**spandrel:** The space between the curves of adjacent arches.

**splayed-foot spire:** If an octagonal spire is placed on a square tower, the corners of the tower will be left uncovered. To resolve this, each intermediate side of a splayed-foot spire is tapered to a point at its base to meet the corner of the tower.

**strapwork:** Style of carved ornament popular in the sixteenth and seventeenth centuries, resembling pierced and interlaced leather straps.

**tester:** Flat canopy above an altar, pulpit, etc.

**tracery:** Moulded bars dividing a window or panel into parts. The successive phases of Gothic architecture can be distinguished by their window-tracery. Trefoil, quatrefoil and sexfoil are lobed tracery shapes, the number of their lobes being three, four and six respectively.

**vault:** Arched roof or ceiling. A barrel vault is semicircular in section; lierne vaulting is composed of intersecting ribs forming decorative star-shaped patterns meeting at bosses (q.v.).

# INDEX